Wedding Anniversaries

FIRST	paper	THIRTEENTH	lace
SECOND	cotton	FOURTEENTH	ivory
THIRD	leather	FIFTEENTH	crystal
FOURTH	linen	TWENTIETH	china
FIFTH	wood	TWENTY-FIFTH	silver
SIXTH	iron	THIRTIETH	pearl
SEVENTH	wool	THIRTY-FIFTH	coral
EIGHTH	bronze	FORTIETH	ruby
NINTH	pottery	FORTY-FIFTH	sapphire
TENTH	tin	FIFTIETH	gold
ELEVENTH	steel	FIFTY-FIFTH	emerald
TWELFTH	silk	SIXTIETH	diamond

Signs of the Zodiac

ARIES   March 21 — April 19

TAURUS   April 20 — May 20

GEMINI   May 21 — June 20

CANCER   June 21 — July 22

LEO   July 23 — August 22

VIRGO   August 23 — September 23

LIBRA   September 24 — October 23

SCORPIO   October 24 — November 21

SAGITTARIUS   November 22 — December 21

CAPRICORN   December 22 — January 19

AQUARIUS   January 20 — February 18

PISCES   February 19 — March 20

Birthstones

JANUARY	garnet
FEBRUARY	amethyst
MARCH	aquamarine
APRIL	diamond
MAY	emerald
JUNE	pearl
JULY	ruby
AUGUST	peridot
SEPTEMBER	sapphire
OCTOBER	opal
NOVEMBER	topaz
DECEMBER	turquoise

January

1

2

3

January

4

5

6

7

January

8

9

10

11

January

12

13

14

15

January

16

17

18

19

January

20

21

22

23

January

24

25

26

27

January

28

29

30

31

February

1

2

3

February

4

5

6

7

February

8

9

10

11

February

12

13

14

15

February

16

17

18

19

February

20

21

22

23

February

24

25

26

27

February

28

29

March

1

2

3

March

4

5

6

7

March

8

9

10

11

March

12

13

14

15

March

16

17

18

19

March

20

21

22

23

March

24

25

26

27

March

28

29

30

31

April

1

2

3

April

4

5

6

7

April

8

9

10

11

April

12

13

14

15

April

16

17

18

19

April

20

21

22

23

April

24

25

26

27

April

28

29

30

May

1

2

3

May

4

5

6

7

May

8

9

10

11

May

12

13

14

15

May

16

17

18

19

May

20

21

22

23

May

24

25

26

27

May

28

29

30

31

June

1

2

3

June

4

5

6

7

June

8

9

10

11

June

12

13

14

15

June

16

17

18

19

June

20

21

22

23

June

24

25

26

27

June

28

29

30

July

1

2

3

July

4

5

6

7

July

8

9

10

11

July

12

13

14

15

July

16

17

18

19

July

20

21

22

23

July

24

25

26

27

July

28

29

30

31

August

1

2

3

August

4

5

6

7

August

8

9

10

11

August

12

13

14

15

August

16

17

18

19

August

20

21

22

23

August

24

25

26

27

August

28

29

30

31

September

_____ 1

_____ 2

_____ 3

September

4

5

6

7

September

8

9

10

11

September

12

13

14

15

September

16

17

18

19

September

20

21

22

23

September

24

25

26

27

September

28

29

30

October

1

2

3

October

4

5

6

7

October

8

9

10

11

October

12

13

14

15

October

16

17

18

19

October

20

21

22

23

October

24

25

26

27

October

28

29

30

31

November

1

2

3

November

4

5

6

7

November

8

9

10

11

November

12

13

14

15

November

16

17

18

19

November

20

21

22

23

November

24

25

26

27

November

28

29

30

December

1

2

3

December

4

5

6

7

December

8

9

10

11

December

12

13

14

15

December

16

17

18

19

December

20

21

22

23

December

24

25

26

27

December

28

29

30

31

Notes

Notes

Notes

Notes

Notes

Notes

Notes

paperstyle

Images taken from *Outdoor Living* by Selina Lake
Photography by Debi Treloar,
copyright © Ryland Peters & Small 2014

Published by Paperstyle
20–21 Jockey's Fields
London WC1R 4BW
and
519 Broadway, 5th Floor
New York, NY 10012
www.rylandpeters.com

10 9 8 7 6 5 4 3 2 1

Text, design and photographs
© Ryland Peters & Small 2014

Printed in China

ISBN: 978-1-84975-523-8